12.95

D0788032

COPING WITH . . .
FOOD
TRASH

▼▼▼▼▼▼▼▼▼▼▼▼▼▼▼▼▼

COPING WITH . . .
FOOD
TRASH

Jamie Daniel • Veronica Bonar
Illustrated by Tony Kenyon

Gareth Stevens Publishing
MILWAUKEE

For a free color catalog describing Gareth Stevens' list of high-quality books, call 1-800-341-3569 (USA) or 1-800-461-9120 (Canada).

Library of Congress Cataloging-in-Publication Data

Daniel, Jamie.
    Coping with— food trash/adapted from Veronica Bonar's Food rubbish! by Jamie Daniel; illustrated by Tony Kenyon. — North American ed.
        p. cm. — (Trash busters)
    Includes bibliographical references and index.
    ISBN 0-8368-1056-2
    1. Organic wastes—Juvenile literature. 2. Food—Juvenile literature. 3. Refuse and refuse disposal—Juvenile literature. [1. Food. 2. Refuse and refuse disposal.] I. Bonar, Veronica. Food rubbish! II. Kenyon, Tony, ill. III. Title. IV. Series: Daniel, Jamie. Trash busters.
TD801.D36   1994
363.72'88--dc20   93-32478

This North American edition first published in 1994 by
Gareth Stevens Publishing
1555 North RiverCenter Drive, Suite 201
Milwaukee, WI 53212, USA

This edition © 1994 by Zoë Books Limited. First produced as *FOOD RUBBISH!*, © 1992 by Zoë Books Limited, original text © 1992 by Veronica Bonar. Additional end matter © 1994 by Gareth Stevens, Inc. Published in the USA by arrangement with Zoë Books Limited, Winchester, England. Published in Canada by arrangement with Heinemann Educational Books Ltd., Oxford, England.

Series editor: Patricia Lantier-Sampon
Cover design: Karen Knutson

Picture Credits:
The Environmental Picture Library p. 24 (G. Glendell); Sally and Richard Greenhill p. 14; Oxford Scientific Films p. 10 (London Scientific Films), p. 13 (Mike Birkhead), p. 20 (Rudie Kuiter), p. 23 (Philip Hart); Science Photo Library p. 18 (Dr. Jeremy Burgess); Zefa pp. 7, 9, 16, 26.

Printed in the USA

1 2 3 4 5 6 7 8 9 99 98 97 96 95 94

At this time, Gareth Stevens, Inc., does not use 100 percent recycled paper, although the paper used in our books does contain about 30 percent recycled fiber. This decision was made after a careful study of current recycling procedures revealed their dubious environmental benefits. We will continue to explore recycling options.

TABLE OF CONTENTS

Words that appear in the glossary are printed in
boldface type the first time they occur in the text.

FOOD AND ENERGY

We use **energy** whenever we do anything. We use it to work, to play, and even to sleep. We get our energy from the foods we eat.

We also need food to grow up strong and healthy. This is why it is important to eat a **balanced diet** — a healthy mixture of different foods.

⬆ This meal of salad, eggs, milk, and whole grain bread is very healthy.

THE FOODS WE EAT

A balanced diet should include **proteins**, **carbohydrates**, and a small amount of fats. Proteins, found in meat, fish, and milk products, build strong bones and muscles. We get carbohydrates from starchy foods like bread and pasta, and from foods containing sugar.

↑ Look at all these healthy foods!

Our bodies also need **vitamins** and **minerals**. Minerals in milk build strong bones. Vitamins in fruits and vegetables help us stay well. We also need **fiber**, which can be found in whole grain breads, fruits, nuts, and other foods.

KEEPING FOOD FRESH

If we store food properly, it stays fresh longer. This way, less food is wasted and thrown away in our trash. If food is left uncovered, **bacteria** in the air cause it to spoil quickly. So it is best to cover uneaten food.

◆ Spoiled food becomes moldy and can't be eaten.

Bacteria spoil food faster when the temperature is warm. If you put food in a refrigerator or other cool place, the bacteria work more slowly, and the food will stay fresh longer. Cooking food is another way to kill some bacteria.

FOOD AND YOUR HEALTH

Good, fresh food keeps us healthy. But we can get sick from eating food that is spoiled. Food also tastes better when it is fresh. Some foods are marked with a date to let you know how long it will be fresh. After this date, the grocer will take it off the shelf.

You should not eat any food after the date printed on the package. It is better to throw it away than risk getting sick.

When you throw food away, wrap it up in paper or a trash bag so insects, mice, and other **pests** won't get into it. Pests can spread dangerous diseases.

↖ If you leave bread or other food out at night, you may attract mice or insects.

FOOD LITTER

When people carelessly throw **litter** on the ground, what they are throwing away is often food packaging. Careless people drop soda cans and hamburger wrappers, and they also drop leftover food. Food litter can attract rats and other disease-carrying pests.

➤ This kind of food litter will be easily found by pests.

Food litter can be dangerous in other ways. People can slip on it and fall. An easy way to avoid these dangers is to wrap your food litter and throw it away in a public garbage can or at home, where you can be certain it won't cause problems.

TRASH FROM FRUITS AND VEGETABLES

Most of the fruits we eat leave only a **core** behind. Most vegetables can be eaten whole, too. In fact, the skins of vegetables, like potatoes and carrots, are full of vitamins. All we need to do is rinse or scrub the skins before eating.

◆ Fresh apples are a good, easy snack.

Even the little bit of waste left when we eat fruits and vegetables can be **recycled**. For example, some vegetable and fruit peels can be used to make jams or soup broth.

Vegetable peels and fruit cores can also be recycled as **compost**. Compost is a material made of decaying plant matter. Adding compost to a garden makes the soil healthier for growing plants.

TRASH FROM MEAT AND FISH

Meat and fish should not be added to a compost pile. Spoiled meat and fish attract pests and can also poison cats and dogs that might eat it.

▲ Flies like this one lay eggs on spoiled meat so the eggs will hatch next to a food source.

Leftover meat and fish have many uses.
For example, they can be added to stews
and soup or used for tacos. There is no
need to throw good meat and fish away!

GETTING RID OF FOOD TRASH

Leftover foods can sometimes be fed to rabbits and guinea pigs. These little animals love fruit and vegetable scraps.

It is also a good idea to leave out suitable leftover foods for birds in winter, such as stale bread, fruits, seeds, or nuts, when it is hard for them to find enough food.

▲ Guinea pigs munch happily on a carrot and an apple.

Cooked foods like gravy or pudding can be safely flushed down the toilet. But most waste food or bones should be wrapped and put in the garbage. Some food garbage is recycled in an unusual way — it is fed to pigs. These animals love to eat fresh garbage.

FOOD WASTE AND OUR DRAINS

Some people who do not have compost heaps use a machine in their sinks called a **garbage disposal** to get rid of food waste. The disposal grinds the food into tiny pieces that are then washed down the drain.

Garbage disposals are helpful because they help lessen the amount of food thrown into trash cans. The ground-up food drains from the kitchen sink into a **sewer** system. **Sewage plants** process the waste to make it less harmful to humans and the environment.

◆ Waste is being treated in round filtering beds at a sewage plant.

WHAT HAPPENS TO OUR TRASH?

In many countries, trash is taken to **landfills**. There, machines called **compactors** squash the trash down so that it will take up less room. Then the trash is buried in the ground so pests like rats won't be able to get to it.

Food that isn't buried will attract pests. The pests can then spread diseases that make other animals and people sick.

◆ A large flock of birds looks for food at this garbage dump.

24

Food trash in older landfills makes a terrible smell as it decays. It also produces a gas called **methane**, which can catch fire easily. Rainwater can seep through rotting trash and flow into streams and rivers to **pollute** the water.

MAKING LESS FOOD TRASH

Some countries get rid of their trash by burning it in big **incinerators**. The trash is burned down to a substance called ash, which can be used to help make roads. Heat from the incinerator can help keep buildings warm or make electricity.

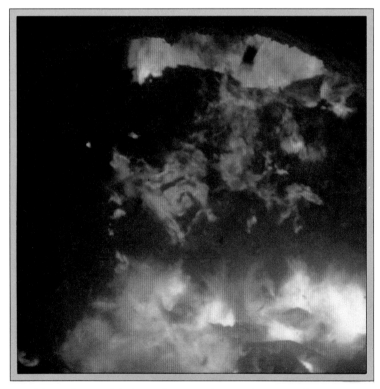

↥ Heat from this burning trash can be used to make electricity.

We will always have to throw away some food. But we often waste food unnecessarily. Sometimes we buy more food than we really need and wind up throwing a lot of it away because it spoils before we can eat it. This is a waste of both good food and money. By watching our eating habits at home and trying not to be wasteful with food and food products, we can stay fit and create less trash.

GLOSSARY

bacteria: tiny creatures in the air, soil, and on plants and animals. Some types of bacteria can break down dead matter or help the body digest food. Other types of bacteria can cause illness.

balanced diet: the right amount of different foods your body needs to stay strong and healthy.

carbohydrates: the substances in some foods that store energy as starch or sugar.

compactors: heavy machines that squash trash together so that it takes up less space.

compost: pieces of fruits, vegetables, and plants that have begun to rot, or decompose, and turn into a rich, soil-like substance. Compost is very good for making soil healthier for growing plants.

core: the center, or middle part, of a fruit, such as an apple or pear. We usually do not eat the core.

energy: the fuel necessary to do work. We eat food to get the energy we need, and machines make energy from fuel to perform tasks.

fiber: any part of food that cannot be broken down by the human body. Fiber passes through the body and helps it digest food.

garbage disposal: a machine built into a sink that can grind food waste into tiny pieces and wash them down the drain.

incinerators: big containers in which trash is burned.

landfill: a big hole in the ground where trash is dumped and then covered with soil.

litter: trash that people carelessly throw on the ground or other places.

methane: a colorless, odorless gas that can be easily burned. Methane can be produced by trash that is buried underground.

minerals: inorganic (non-living) elements found in foods that help keep bodies healthy. Iron and calcium are two minerals that are good for healthy bodies.

pests: Animals that cause damage to other living things. Some pests attracted by uncovered trash are rats, mice, and flies.

pollute: to put harmful materials into the soil, water, or air.

proteins: substances in some foods that help build muscle tissue and repair the body.

recycle: to make a new product from an old product that has already been used. Many metal, food, glass, and paper products can be recycled.

sewage plants: places where waste water and other waste matter from homes and businesses are treated and cleaned.

sewer: a system of pipes, usually underground, that carries waste water and other waste matter to a sewage plant.

vitamins: chemical substances found in food that are necessary to keep bodies strong and healthy. The lack of certain vitamins can lead to disease. A well-balanced diet with plenty of fresh fruits, vegetables, and dairy products usually provides all the vitamins the body needs.

PLACES TO WRITE

Here are some places you can write for more information about trash and recycling. Be sure to give your name and address, and be clear about what you would like to know. Include a stamped, self-addressed envelope for a reply.

Greenpeace Foundation
   (Canada)
185 Spadina Avenue
Sixth Floor
Toronto, Ontario
M5T 2C6

Institute of Scrap Recycling
   Industries
1325 G Street NW
Suite 1000
Washington, D.C. 20005

The National Recycling
   Coalition
1101 30th Street NW
Suite 305
Washington, D.C. 20007

INTERESTING FACTS ABOUT FOOD

Did you know . . .

▶ that in the days before refrigeration, people used to preserve meat by treating it with salt, pepper, and other spices?

▶ that a few foods taste better once they start to get moldy? Some types of cheese, like blue cheese, need a little mold to give them their flavor.

▶ that raw food and cooked food should never be stored in the same container? This is because bacteria easily pass from one food to the other.

▶ that you can do your part to help cut down on food waste by putting only as much food on your plate at a meal as you think you can really eat? Remember, you can probably ask for a second helping!

▶ that about 35 percent of our garbage is food waste?

MORE BOOKS TO READ

Cartons, Cans, and Orange Peels: Where Does Our Garbage Go?
   Joanna Foster (Houghton Mifflin)

Domestic Waste. Tony Hare (Watts)

Earthwise at Home: A Guide to the Care and Feeding of Your Planet.
   Linda Lowery (Carolrhoda Books)

Reducing, Reusing, and Recycling. Bobby Kalman (Crabtree)

Stop That Garbage Truck! Linda Glaser (A. Whitman)

Where Does Garbage Go? Isaac Asimov (Gareth Stevens)

INDEX